MADIBAKWENA
MOTIVATIONAL POEMS

BY

MAMADIBA LYDIA PHALOANE &
KWENA GRANNY MPHELA

To order additional copies of this book, contact:
Xlibris
UK TFN: 0800 0148620 (Toll Free inside the UK)
UK Local: 02036 956328 (+44 20 3695 6328 from outside the UK)
www.xlibrispublishing.co.uk
Orders@ Xlibrispublishing.co.uk

ISBN: Softcover 978-1-4628-6560-4
EBook 978-1-6641-1256-8

Print information available on the last page

Rev. date: 09/01/2020

PREFACE

This is a highly spiritual book meant for self motivation and inspiration by any individual in circumstances which he or she does not feel comfortable with, or not coping with. When reading the book, know for certain that by using your faith and the power in you by virtue of you being made in the image of the almighty, you are bound to yield good results. The good result is the new you. The book is based on the power of the magic number 3 manifesting itself in the miracle from the holy cross. The cross characterized by its three pins in the form of A TRIANGLE FACING DOWN. This is the rational behind the South African flag watermark on some of the pages of the book "with a black triangle facing down". Each poem is followed by a therapeutic exercise in the form of a table that allows you to elicite both the undesirable aspects matching them with the desirable and positive aspects to help create the new you. The last part is a powerful exercise where you collate all positive aspects and write 4 stories or poems about the new you. The images that precede each new poem and story have their own story to tell and inspire you.

At the beginning, when reading and finally compiling your own story you are encouraged to read the words below. If you know of any South African (Black), contact him/her to learn the tune of this powerful hymn sang for more that 200 years by all Africans as their solace and source of strength. The hymn:"BODIBENG BA MAHLOMOLA MOO KE NENG KE TEBILE.HA KESE KEYA TIMELA. MORENA JESU ONA NKGOPOLA.WA HLAHA WA NTUTUBOLLA.KA TSOTA DINTLE TSA HAE. KA TSEBA LE HO NYAKALLA HOBA KE BONE MOHAU".KE NNA YA LEFANG TSWHARELO. KENNA YA LE FODISANG.MORENA HA ORIALO REKA BELAELA JWANG." **The literal meaning is that**:" WHEN I WAS DROWNING IN TRIALS AND TRIBULATIONS. JUST WHEN I THOUGHT MY LIFE WAS OVER.YOU LORD JESUS CAME AND RESCUED ME.I THEN KNEW HOW TO BE HAPPY.I THEN BECAME CONCIOUS OF THE BEAUTY OF YOUR CREATION BECAUSE OF YOUR GRACE.

ACKNOWLEDGEMENTS

Who else can I express my greatest gratitude to if not my creator who made me to be a creative artist in the form of writing African and gospel music, poetry and motivational speeches? Another set of heartfelt thanks go to my 16 year old daughter and 26 year old niece who read the manuscript in its earliest form and were impressed. Also to my late brother's daughter who was brave enough to disclose her HIV status and allowed me to write a poem about her courage and zest for life after her diagnosis. I cannot forget the late Mr. Kananda who was my grade 9 English teacher and principal. He was one of the best well spoken English teacher in the Vaal/Gauteng province, South Africa. He gave me a nickname: "TEASPOON" for being petite yet always leading with results, English in particular. Lastly my late parents who gave me a very solid background as Christians and education loving couple with leadership qualities utilized in church and within the larger community. They surely are proud of this book in their spirit world as angels in heaven. Good News Bible, Matthew 1, Lord Jesus acknowledges his ancestors. As a proud Christian I wish to acknowledge my paternal and maternal ancestors too by saying their African praise song:" The daughter of Mariha.Ubungane, Mthimkhulu, Radebe, ndlebe zi khanya ilanga umashwabada ushwabada inkomo nempondo zayo. Umfazi webele elide uncelisa umtwana phesheya kwemfula! Setloholo sa Mapela, matebele a matle a laka. Langalibalele. Dododo zithi mpe. Dotlou tse kgolo!

OUT OF THE CLOSET OUT OF THE CLOAK

Out of the closet for the universe to see, admire and honor. Yes! Me covered in the cloak of HIV and AIDS. The day of my unveiling has dawned! Covered in veil like a newly erected tombstone. Wrapped with a red ribbon like a gift box. And then the world asked why the red ribbon? Yes ! It had to be a red ribbon, the natural color of blood. Like breast milk, the blood that feeds this pandemic, to ensure its growth and nourishment. Not an ordinary ribbon it is. But the umbilical cord that tied victims like me ,you and others to this pandemic. When the universe trembled in fear, seeing it as a monster. I, on this day woke up with smiles on my face knowing it is the celebration of my unveiling! Like doctors at the ecstasy of joy, cutting the baby's umbilical cord. Why the excitement ? It is the joy of knowing that the day has dawned for the baby to be independent from its mother. The beginning of new life outside the cocoon of the tummy, into the sunshine for the world to see and admire. Impatiently asking: "Is it a boy or a girl?" Regardless of the sex. It is a bouncy baby, the universe has been awaiting.

Copy cats are the middle names of mankind. A trend it has become ,for mankind to mimic the cutting of the ribbon in all unveilings. Opening new doors for the universe to admire what is inside. Yes it is you and me coming out of the cloak of secrecy, non disclosure and saying to the people come into our new life as victims. Admire the imported furniture. My new self confidence, self esteem ,my strength. Yes! The new me.

Like a new bridge that has been let loose off the red ribbon being unveiled, I come out ready to stand the test of time. The test of the manmade storms of rejection, shame and scornful attitudes. That's what bridges are for anyway. Made to either be stamped on or make way for mankind to cross over to the other side of the road. To the destination of empathy and not sympathy. For the ribbon, the umbilical cord around me has been cut and I have outgrown the cloak of self pity. You too shall outgrow it!

When reading the book:

USE THE POWER OF THE TRIANGLE
TO REGENERATE THE NEW YOU.

Meditate and listen to:.

1. Holy Voice of the Lord
2. Your inner voice
3. The tranquility
and sounds
of nature

READER EXCERSISE:

LIST 9 FACTORS OR WORDS FROM THE POEM THAT REPRESENT YOUR UNDESIRABLE / SAD CIRCUMSTANCES. READ THE POEM AGAIN AND THEN MATCH THOSE WORDS WITH POSITIVE/INSPIRATIONAL WORDS FROM THE POEM. READ OVER AND OVER AGAIN UNTIL YOU HAVE AN EQUAL NUMBER ON BOTH SIDES OF THE TABLE.

1.	1.
2.	2.
3.	3.
4.	4.
5.	5.
6.	6.
7.	7.
8.	8.
9.	9.

MY HIVE MY LIFE

When the universe expects me to be overpowered by its stereotype ,my heart pumped, raising my high blood pressure. For my mind could not take the pressure of the cowardice that is torturing mankind. My life is an open book for the vulnerable world to read and become strong like I am. For I am the product of the powerful letter "E". The heir to Mother Eve in the garden of Eden. Through the heavenly wisdom I invited this letter into my life and transformed the meaning of the HIV monster into HIVE.I then declared my HIV life my BEE HIVE.

Man, women, children of Africa listen to my words of wisdom. For my wisdom cometh from two powerful women. My late mother and my late paternal grand mother. By virtue of them being born in a village called Evaton, they are products of Eve. The heavenly wisdom whispered to them saying the "ton" letter in the name Evaton means "tuin", the garden. Yes Evaton, the garden of Eve called Eden, where life originates sayeth the holy book. The garden that provides food for thought. If only mankind could give an ear to my word of wisdom. For it is the truth. No wonder the two products of Eve named me Ruth. Yes Ruth the HIV Positive African Woman holding the knife on its sharp side. For the monster not to cut vulnerable mankind but fruits, vegetables and herbs from the garden of Eve. Where else can one find a bee HIV"E "if not in an orchard the powerful generator of new life. The HIV that gave me new life characterized by "E"verlasting peace of mind after I chose to add the E letter into my life. My HIVE my life.

My newly defined life that I have declared to make it an open book for the world to witness how I bravely uprooted the bee sting. Uprooted the painful needle of the HIV monster plunged into my body like an uninvited guest. Mankind ask me where I got the bravery from. Where else if not from the African name that I am proud of:" Malehlohonolo "meaning Blessing. What a combination of the two names Ruth Malehlohonolo. The heavenly planned names that say to the vulnerable and fearful world:" My life is an open book of truth and blessing" For my new HIV life is meant to Bless the vulnerable people of the universe. For it is the gospel truth, that I AM HIV POSITIVE AND PROUDLY LIVING WITH IT UNTIL I HOLD MY GRAND CHILDREN IN MY ARMS. You too can make the same declaration.

When reading the book:

USE THE POWER OF THE TRIANGLE
TO REGENERATE THE NEW YOU.

Meditate and listen to:.

1. Holy Voice of the Lord
2. Your inner voice
3. The tranquility
   and sounds
   of nature

READER EXCERSISE:

LIST 9 FACTORS OR WORDS FROM THE POEM THAT REPRESENT YOUR UNDESIRABLE / SAD CIRCUMSTANCES. READ THE POEM AGAIN AND THEN MATCH THOSE WORDS WITH POSITIVE/INSPIRATIONAL WORDS FROM THE POEM. READ OVER AND OVER AGAIN UNTIL YOU HAVE AN EQUAL NUMBER ON BOTH SIDES OF THE TABLE.

1.	1.
2.	2.
3.	3.
4.	4.
5.	5.
6.	6.
7.	7.
8.	8.
9.	9.

FEAR

By faith I shall walk the talk just like my hero Dr Rolihlahla Nelson Mandela who took the first bold step from prison to presidency. As of now, I am taking the first step out of my cocoon, my bedroom which I have turned into my hiding place into the outside world to face it with bold eyes.

For how long will my ears be filled with shouts of counselors, the government and concerned Africans saying to me, you are still one of us. Come out and receive unconditional love and acceptance.

The book of life says I was fearfully and wonderfully created by the almighty. Who should I therefore fear?

*I just heard a tiny voice from my guardian angel giving me the power to change the word fear, rename it and give it new meaning: **F**oolish **EAR**.*

It then stands to reason that only a foolish ear ignores echoes of the words of wisdom from one wise man who once said:" Cowards die many times before their actual death." I AM NO COWARD and therefore will not die before my actual death.

I, on the contrary am stepping into new life of boldness. For greater are the opportunities awaiting me outside my bedroom, my hiding place.

If not into the accepting hands of the nation, I am coming out to fall into my own hands of self determination. So determined to move on with my life.

No longer am I a stagnant dam but have been mobilized into becoming a running river. And not long I shall be the vibrant ocean. The ocean that connects the continents and islands of the universe.

Who then are these continents and the islands if not those people who are still isolated from the nation, their fellow brothers and sisters? For they are still battling with the paralysis of the monster which they haven't renamed. The monster that I previously called fear BUT NOT ANYMORE.

When reading the book:

USE THE POWER OF THE TRIANGLE
TO REGENERATE THE NEW YOU.

Meditate and listen to:.

1. Holy Voice of the Lord
2. Your inner voice
3. The tranquility
and sounds
of nature

READER EXCERSISE:

LIST 9 FACTORS OR WORDS FROM THE POEM THAT REPRESENT YOUR UNDESIRABLE /
SAD CIRCUMSTANCES. READ THE POEM AGAIN AND THEN MATCH THOSE WORDS WITH
POSITIVE/INSPIRATIONAL WORDS FROM THE POEM. READ OVER AND OVER AGAIN
UNTIL YOU HAVE AN EQUAL NUMBER ON BOTH SIDES OF THE TABLE.

1.	1.
2.	2.
3.	3.
4.	4.
5.	5.
6.	6.
7.	7.
8.	8.
9.	9.

IF ONLY YOU COULD SMILE

Just smile when the world expects you to sigh! Instill new meaning and new shape to your life. Like the sun that comes and goes, giving new meaning to daily life. Giving each of the four corners of mother earth changing meaning.

__At dawn__, the first corner when life begins to thrive, echoes of melodies from smiling birds waking mankind from his bed. __Morning__ ,when the sun rays go up melting the morning dew that fills up and gives life to running rivers and streams. Melting and maneuvering deep beneath the soil to fill up underground waters where it belongs. __Noon__, when the full sunshine commands you to nourish your life with a smile on your face for the sun itself is smiling to the world saying:" Let your eyeballs be opened to their fullest capacity for them to admire the beauty of nature and the beauty in you.

By virtue of you being a natural being ,you inherently possess that beauty. Therefore, expect no appreciation from mankind for that beauty. Instead, let self praise be the order of your everyday saying to the world:"I shall on a daily basis enjoy my natural outside and inner beauty equally. The last corner of the setting sun called the __night__. When evil rejoices, awaiting darkness, expecting me to toss and turn imprisoned by depression and sleeplessness. I then opened my eyeballs wide in that darkness and shouted:"NOT ANYMORE!" You are used to me waking up swimming in tears. Not anymore for I now wake up soaring in heights like an eagle that soars better in stormy weathers. Now my destiny is the peak of the mountain where eagles rest. My destiny, my peace of mind for I no longer reserve the place to host sadness, depression and self defeating emotional state. I am too beautiful for words. A smiling face I shall ever portray for the world to admire this heavenly bestowed beauty that no man can take away.

The world shall in return smile with me for having scratched its back with my smile in the midst of tribulations, practically living the African proverb that says :"Fa ofa fi!", I scratch your back you scratch mine!

When reading the book:

USE THE POWER OF THE TRIANGLE
TO REGENERATE THE NEW YOU.

Meditate and listen to:.

1. Holy Voice of the Lord
2.Your inner voice
3. The tranquility
and sounds
of nature

READER EXCERSISE:

LIST 9 FACTORS OR WORDS FROM THE POEM THAT REPRESENT YOUR UNDESIRABLE / SAD CIRCUMSTANCES. READ THE POEM AGAIN AND THEN MATCH THOSE WORDS WITH POSITIVE/INSPIRATIONAL WORDS FROM THE POEM.READ OVER AND OVER AGAIN UNTIL YOU HAVE AN EQUAL NUMBER ON BOTH SIDES OF THE TABLE.

1.	1.
2.	2.
3.	3.
4.	4.
5.	5.
6.	6.
7.	7.
8.	8.
9.	9.

DOWN SPIRITED!

I woke up one day feeling down. Not only down but down spirited! Evil thoughts and the evil spirit then said :" You are down and out! Out of the books of happiness, bright future and life as a whole! And so was my heart convinced. Fountains filling up with tears rolling from my cheeks. Drowning in the ocean of self pity. Waves of sea water written:" bleak future, sadness, sorrow", was all I could see.

I saw myself helplessly sinking deeper and deeper in the ocean of hopelessness. Echoes of the enemy saying :"You will not survive this fatal water nor the predators of the deep ocean." Listening with the second ear, the spiritual ear. I then realized I have been given the second chance in life. I could then hear the spirit of Ubuntu echoing the powerful words that say:" You are a born worrier. By virtue of you being a worrier, you belong to the soil, the earth and the ground. Lying down to hide from the enemy is eminent." Spontaneously, the worrier 's knees go down, letting the body lie flat . The only best position to plan the attack of the enemy. The position that maintains one's contact with mother earth, the soil that is the source of inspiration and revitalization. It stands to reason that mankind cannot live without it.For he is the direct product of the soil and dust. Suddenly, I then realized the value of the soil, from which the underground water ,plants and precious stones are all cultivated .

How else does mankind receive these natural benefits, if not through life throwing one down on the ground, knowing that I shall wake up not empty handed. The enemy would then wonder how I got revitalized. And the answer would be: "I am a worrier that belongs to the ground." A worrier that conquered the enemy called sadness, hopelessness and sorrow whilst lying down." Down spirited I had to be, for the Spirit of Ubuntu to be in touch with my soul and lift me to be a conqueror with everlasting internal peace!

When reading the book:

USE THE POWER OF THE TRIANGLE
TO REGENERATE THE NEW YOU.

Meditate and listen to:.

1. Holy Voice of the Lord
2.Your inner voice
3. The tranquility
and sounds
of nature

READER EXCERSISE:

LIST 9 FACTORS OR WORDS FROM THE POEM THAT REPRESENT YOUR UNDESIRABLE /
SAD CIRCUMSTANCES. READ THE POEM AGAIN AND THEN MATCH THOSE WORDS WITH
POSITIVE/INSPIRATIONAL WORDS FROM THE POEM.READ OVER AND OVER AGAIN
UNTIL YOU HAVE AN EQUAL NUMBER ON BOTH SIDES OF THE TABLE.

1.	1.
2.	2.
3.	3.
4.	4.
5.	5.
6.	6.
7.	7.
8.	8.
9.	9.

MORE THAN A PRAYER

It took more than a prayer for the Israelites to be released from Egypt. Out of the lifelong bondage. It took the Almighty's physical efforts to shake the solid heart of Pharaoh. It took the blood shed of sheep to mark the doors of Israelites for the angel of death to pass to the unmarked doors and do the Almighty's will. It took the miracle of touching all sizes of the Egyptians wooden sticks and Moses' stick that turned into a snake that swallowed all other snakes. It took Israelites stay without food for sometime hence Christians believe in the power of fasting. You too the African Traditional healers. It took walking on foot towards the red sea no wonder you African churches and healers feel that power when dancing all night long, glorifying heaven, the holy place of the Almighty, black ancestors and white ancestors. Ancestors who are angels that have and will forever communicate heavenly messages to us on earth.

Through visions, dreams and their tiny voices. It took the touching of the vibrant red sea by father Moses with his rod for the bloody sea water to fearfully make guard of honor to the Israelites creating dry path. And when the enemy took it for granted that the honor was for them too, to their utter amazement they were finished, swallowed by the red sea. So shall it be with your heavy laden life, tortured by unbearable tribulations. Hard for you to open your eyes from the swelling of ever dripping tears. Hush! Slowly open them and beg them to dry up. For you have embarked on the banks of your breakthrough. Walking on dry land, being honored by those tribulations. Off your shoulders they now walk beside you, giving you standing ovation like the red sea that gave way.

The power of its blood you felt from the time your ancestors taught you that water and blood together have healing powers like they healed Israelites from fatal fear of the enemy behind. No wonder traditionally, Africans silently slaughter and let the blood mingle with holy water in the rivers, for the nation to be healed.

When reading the book:

USE THE POWER OF THE TRIANGLE
TO REGENERATE THE NEW YOU.

Meditate and listen to:.

1. Holy Voice of the Lord
2. Your inner voice
3. The tranquility
and sounds
of nature

READER EXCERSISE:

LIST 9 FACTORS OR WORDS FROM THE POEM THAT REPRESENT YOUR UNDESIRABLE /
SAD CIRCUMSTANCES. READ THE POEM AGAIN AND THEN MATCH THOSE WORDS WITH
POSITIVE/INSPIRATIONAL WORDS FROM THE POEM.READ OVER AND OVER AGAIN
UNTIL YOU HAVE AN EQUAL NUMBER ON BOTH SIDES OF THE TABLE.

1.	1.
2.	2.
3.	3.
4.	4.
5.	5.
6.	6.
7.	7.
8.	8.
9.	9.

THE MUSHROOMING HERBS

For the love of money, the old stealing tendencies got resurrected ! The tendency of putting a smile on the face whilst stealing our land, wisdom and wealth. Not realizing that Africans are still chanting their ancestral songs of Ubuntu, the spirit of togetherness. No longer political songs with tears but echoing the song that says. We were once blind but now we can see and forever shall keep our eyes open. Once bitten twice shine!

Brainwashed against the holy voice of our ancestors. Fear of demonic spirit instilled in our innocent minds. Yet that voice has been and remains holy. Giving mankind wisdom to invent and earn a living. Least did we Africans know that our wisdom was being stoically stolen and wealth created from it. Made to hold on to the unethical notion that ancestors and the Bible don't belong together. Who then is Father David, Father Solomon, Father Abraham no longer in this world and the list is endless? Are they not the white ancestors whose voice guides the technology, inventions and wealth of the white nation from the time of the Bible, to date? If any man can say this aint true. Then why not change the old names of businesses named after white ancestors who no longer belong to this world? Yes! Ancient business names retained for fear of communication breakdown with those founder members.

*Lest the heirs to those estates no longer will they receive messages about new inventions on annual basis and down the drain will those business ventures go. No wonder the companies annual Christmas parties and business launching ceremonies. How else will they communicate with and thank their business fountains, their ancestors. Braai smoke and three sips of wine??? The bold writing is vivid on the wall for us to see! Yet we Africans have been made to frown at and not honor our forefathers. Beware of your intellectual property, your traditional, herbal medicine wisdom! Why all the scientific enquiry and the remarkable interest in our so called demonic medicine. The commercialization of our ancestors herbs and the mushrooming companies. All in the name of wealth continually stolen from us. For once, let the Africans human right to uninterrupted wealth **be respected!***

When reading the book:

USE THE POWER OF THE TRIANGLE
TO REGENERATE THE NEW YOU.

Meditate and listen to:.

1. Holy Voice of the Lord
2. Your inner voice
3. The tranquility
and sounds
of nature

READER EXCERSISE:

LIST 9 FACTORS OR WORDS FROM THE POEM THAT REPRESENT YOUR UNDESIRABLE /
SAD CIRCUMSTANCES. READ THE POEM AGAIN AND THEN MATCH THOSE WORDS WITH
POSITIVE/INSPIRATIONAL WORDS FROM THE POEM.READ OVER AND OVER AGAIN
UNTIL YOU HAVE AN EQUAL NUMBER ON BOTH SIDES OF THE TABLE.

1.	1.
2.	2.
3.	3.
4.	4.
5.	5.
6.	6.
7.	7.
8.	8.
9.	9.

THE BEE HIVE

Like a bee, so painfully it stings, waiting for that moment where you are at your deepest tranquility, drowning in your inner happiness! At the pick of genuine contentment, saying to yourself:"All is well!". Everything portraying peace and harmony!

At the time you feel your future is in your capable hands. Everything remarkably under your control. Flying high in the sky of ambition. Breathing the breeze of tangible life possibilities and ripe opportunities, ready to touch your palate, and then its unbearable pain coming from its cruel venomous needle pricks your balloon of hope for air to escape.

And when it was rejoicing, imagining the air of hope and ambition leaving this balloon called your soul. To its utter amazement and dismay, there echoed a tiny voice saying behold it is not ordinary air but....?

Pollution of new life as I plug out that venomous needle. New blood oozing from the wound yet it brought new meaning. Suddenly I found myself landing from one flower to another. Eating pollen of care and love from doctors, care givers and the community. I woke up singing the new song that says:" Suddenly life has new meaning of greater hope for survival and there is beauty up above! Filled with smiles I then vowed to cross pollinate the zest to move on with life. Transfer it to those who believe it is the end. Raising their eyes in the air they then will see my pollen written all over. On the contrary saying:" It is the beginning. Time to build more BEE HIVES to feed the hungry nation with new honey. No HIVE, no honey!

How sweet the world would end up being. Sweetened by the honey stored in us the world's new BEE HIVES. No longer tortured by the monster called HIV but embracing the fact that honey preserves life and being carriers of this virus we are here to build more HIVES for more lives to be preserved.

When reading the book:

USE THE POWER OF THE TRIANGLE
TO REGENERATE THE NEW YOU.

Meditate and listen to:.

1. Holy Voice of the Lord
2.Your inner voice
3. The tranquility
and sounds
of nature

READER EXCERSISE:

LIST 9 FACTORS OR WORDS FROM THE POEM THAT REPRESENT YOUR UNDESIRABLE /
SAD CIRCUMSTANCES. READ THE POEM AGAIN AND THEN MATCH THOSE WORDS WITH
POSITIVE/INSPIRATIONAL WORDS FROM THE POEM.READ OVER AND OVER AGAIN
UNTIL YOU HAVE AN EQUAL NUMBER ON BOTH SIDES OF THE TABLE.

1.	1.
2.	2.
3.	3.
4.	4.
5.	5.
6.	6.
7.	7.
8.	8.
9.	9.

THE NEW ME : MY STORY. MY POEM

To you the reader: Clay is soil and you the reader are a product of the soil. Use the power of the magic number 3 once more. Inside these three calabashes is where your renewed strength is stored. Lord Jesus once used clay pots too. (Revelations 22: 2) The tree of life has green leaves yielding ripe yellow fruits throughout the year. Enjoy what the renewed life offers you as fruits on a daily basis

Let your story be guided by the next 4 images and their inspirational messages. Also refer back to the tables you made about each of these 4 selected poems. Your book must have your own new story written with your own hand. This is the only way to feel tangible results. You shall have achieved your goal. This tool kit shall have achieved the purpose it is meant for. Thank you and BE EMOTIONALLY HEALED.BE HAPPY AND BE GRATEFUL FOR THE NEW YOU!

OUT OF THE CLOSET OUT OF THE CLOAK

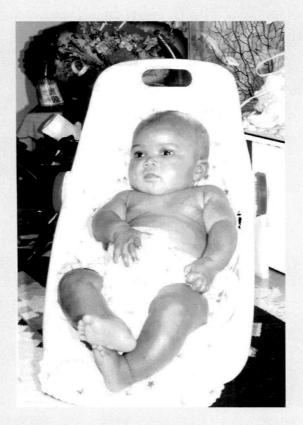

To you the reader. The umbilical cord cut for the baby to be independent from the mother. This baby is now 16 year old. She stood the test of time of severe allergy that left many doctors confused every time HIV test results came back negative yet her condition appeared like a fully blown AIDS. Doctors' remarks would always be:" This is a child with remarkable willpower. Her faith from childhood made her overcome death every time she got hospitalized".

Let your story be guided by the next 4 images and their inspirational messages. Also refer back to the tables you made about each of these 4 selected poems. Your book must have your own new story written with your own hand. This is the only way to feel tangible results. You shall have achieved your goal. This tool kit shall have achieved the purpose it is meant for. Thank you and BE EMOTIONALLY HEALED.BE HAPPY AND BE GRATEFUL FOR THE NEW YOU!

IF ONLY I COULD SMILE

To you the reader. Change the word "you" to "I" in the poem "If only you could smile"when creating your own poem. Do so whilst forcing yourself to smile in front of a mirror and generate positive, inspirational words. Refer to this image because Smile is infactious.Feel the immediate impact on your emotions.Do it .It has worked in many therapy sessions conducted by the author Mamadiba as a social worker and counselor.

Let your story be guided by the next 4 images and their inspirational messages. Also refer back to the tables you made about each of these 4 selected poems. Your book must have your own new story written with your own hand. This is the only way to feel tangible results. You shall have achieved your goal. This tool kit shall have achieved the purpose it is meant for. Thank you and BE EMOTIONALLY HEALED.BE HAPPY AND BE GRATEFUL FOR THE NEW YOU!

THE BEE HIVE

To you the reader. Take yourself as that bee taking pollen from one flower to the next to make a difference in your life and the lives of others. Shift focus from self pity and do one good thing for someone on a daily basis no matter how small. As small as making somebody laugh even though you yourself are in pain or sorrow.

Let your story be guided by the next 4 images and their inspirational messages. Also refer back to the tables you made about each of these 4 selected poems. Your book must have your own new story written with your own hand. This is the only way to feel tangible results. You shall have achieved your goal. This tool kit shall have achieved the purpose it is meant for. Thank you and BE EMOTIONALLY HEALED.BE HAPPY AND BE GRATEFUL FOR THE NEW YOU!

DOWN SPIRITED

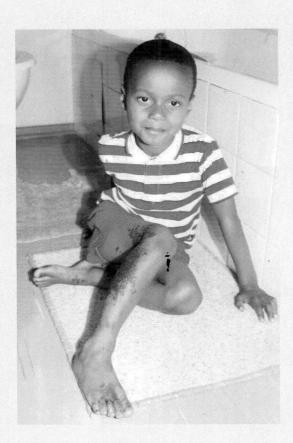

To you the reader. The boy stood the test of a possible leg amputation at 9 years. For months he could not walk but crawl because the injury had affected his knee muscles. By the GRACE OF THE LIVING ALMIGHTY he still has his leg at 23 years in 2011. Write about the Grace in your life and claim victory over your circumstances.

Printed in the United States
By Bookmasters